Grin & Bare It

Rants of a Single, Non-Lesbian Woman over 40

_____

Colleen Clement

MARSHALL - MICHIGAN
800PUBLISHING.COM

Grin & Bare It

Copyright © 2011 by Colleen Clement

Cover design by   2 Moon Press
                    307 W. Michigan Ave., Marshall MI 49068
                    800publishing.com

Author photo by   Courtesy of Author

ISBN-13: 978-1-935805-98-4
ISBN-10:

First published in 2010

10 9 8 7 6 5 4 3 2 1

Published by   2 MOON PRESS
                  Marshall, Michigan
                  www.800publishing.com

Acknowledgments

A special thanks…

- to my friends Natalie and Amy for their extra help in getting me to finish this darn thing!
- to my parents, Mary Lou and Jim, who raised me in a loving environment, encouraging strength of character, seeking truth, and trusting divine guidance.

About the Author:

Originally from a small town in southwest Michigan, Colleen recently earned a Masters in Drama and Theatre for the Young from Eastern Michigan University. She's currently working on her doctorate from the University of Victoria in British Columbia, Canada.

Grin & Bare It

Rants of a Single, Non-Lesbian Woman over 40

Someone just like me is out there who wants to know that she/he is not alone in feeling like the outsider...so far outside of the box...a box that you didn't know existed until one day it hits you like a brick. Actually, no, it doesn't hit you. No, you run into it...run right into the invisible outside wall of the box. And you're like, "What the frick?!" You feel like an idiot for running into something, like tripping on the sidewalk and looking back to see what that heck made you jerk forward so hard while everyone else is laughing. Do you know what I mean?

I gotta believe there is one person out there in our seven billion or so person world who gets that. Now, mind you, this box wasn't placed there intentionally to make people miserable and feel excluded. No...I'm convinced it started with good intentions, but we all know where those get you, right? I'm telling you, that's the one piece of wisdom that never made much sense to me as a kid, but Holy Crap, it certainly does now.

Many a road to our personal Hells has been paved with the ever well-meaning Good Intention. It's one sneaky, little, seductive force that intention, too, used for eons as the excuse for something that has clearly gone astray from the original intent. For example, many of our society's traditions supposedly celebrate love. A noble idea. I'm all for love. But these traditions developed into really limited acceptable formats...you know...concrete categories of love and ranking of love...like one form of love is somehow greater than another. And it was a slippery slope from there...

Chapter 1
Where to start?

Let me begin with a delightful little story. I decided a few years ago to go back to school. Just had to jump off the work carousel, you know? I was very proud of myself for the opportunities I took advantage of in the program, including a trip to the Netherlands for a theater internship. I had never been there and the theater never had an intern from the US. No one else in my program was going, so I went solo. I was totally nervous but thrilled at the same time to be observing a company that does superior puppetry work. I didn't know anyone there personally. I arrived on a Friday so that I would be fresh to start on Monday. Exciting, right?!

Well, a woman from the theater met me on Saturday for coffee to welcome me to the theater. Not even five minutes into the conversation, this woman could no longer hold back her burning question. Did she want to know what brought me to puppetry at this point in my life? Nope. Why I left behind the corporate world? Nuh-uh. Much more pressing than that. Ready? Here goes...totally off topic she blurts out, "Do you mind if I ask you a personal question? Do you like women?" Yep. You heard me right. "Do you like women?" Are you kidding me?! Apparently that's the only way she could rationalize my traveling by myself to another country and why I, as a 44-year old woman, wasn't married.

I think I was actually stunned that a theater person, of all people, from a famously liberal country no less, gave a rat's rectum about my sexual orientation. I was just sipping a cappuccino while nibbling on a side of jet lag. It's not like I was hitting on her or vice versa. I could only laugh. I didn't even know this woman, and this was a primary concern for her. She was married and had a couple of grandkids. I guess her only explanation for me being alone was that I was a lesbian. Now, correct me if I'm wrong, but doesn't being a lesbian have a little to do with what gender you like to have sex with and *not* whether or not you're single? Or maybe it was because I dared fly alone to a foreign country? That could be it. Interestingly enough, most of my homosexual women friends are actually in a coupled scenario at the moment, so perhaps I need to ask them about their travel preferences.

And what if I were a lesbian? Exactly how would that have changed the scenario for this woman? Did it have any bearing on the purpose of my internship? Would it have severely augmented my level of talent as it relates to theater? Would she have suddenly said, "That's what I suspected. We're gonna have to adjust our internship schedule. This changes everything."?

Now, I happen to think it was pretty darn cool that I arranged to receive graduate credit for *not* sitting in a classroom, for traveling to a beautiful country where I'd never been and they spoke a language different from my own, for meeting some incredibly talented people, and for opening my horizons farther than this small Midwestern town girl ever thought possible. And yes, I went...all by myself! Now if that makes me a lesbian, then so be it. And if it does, then there are an awful lot of men who travel alone, so I guess they must be lesbians, too. Am I the only one who sees this as just a tad silly, not to mention just plain insulting to lesbians everywhere to equate them with some sort of default setting for those of us apparently seen as sadly and desperately alone?

And can I just point something out? Since when did being single have any to do with homosexuality? When did being married stop anyone from being gay? Seriously. When?

Yes, there are times when it can be highly festive to travel around with someone, but that's not because I'm single. It's because it can be fun hanging out with people, sharing experiences. However, there are plenty of times when I enjoy my solitude. I especially love seeing certain movies all by myself, like epic adventures...you know...the ones where you can take a journey to a faraway place without worrying what anybody else around you thinks. Sometimes you just need your own private time. Do I really have to feel somehow lesser because I am not partnered with someone every second of my life?

So I now declare that, yes, I am a single, heterosexual woman over 40, damn it! Just trying to hack out an existence on my own in this world of supposed-to's and should-be's. Venting...sharing my rants with you in hopes of making someone laugh a little and not feel so alone as we examine some of the boundaries in our modern society. Life's not always an easy journey for anyone...single or coupled. Believe me, if I thought it would make things easier, I'd take a crack at lesbianism, but, alas, I don't have that luxury. I didn't choose this! I was born this way. And you know...*you know* there's some staunch homophobe out there thinking, "Poor thing. Probably would be so much easier if she was a lez." You know it!

It's very strange to be part of a subclass that's forever speculated about like a half-human creature lurking in the bowels of an opera house or something. Actually, it's not too bad until you start approaching 40, sans ring on finger, that is. "There must be something wrong with her." "Why hasn't she met anyone yet?" "She must be a lesbian." Shhhhhhh!!!

What is up with our society? We tell people to follow their heart, their dreams, not to settle, and yet we limit what that is supposed to look like to that of being married by this time and kids by that time. Must everyone follow the same path to love? Must everyone be part of a couple at every moment of their lives to have love in their lives? Why do we cling so strongly via our traditions and mass media to one picture of love when we know beyond a shadow of a doubt that not all couples are loving or even close to it? Why do we throw pity on a person who has followed her heart, has had incredible experiences and friends in her life, has not committed to someone who wanted her to be less than who she is, and who loves who she is and what she has learned, knowing that *all* relationships present themselves at the perfect time for the perfect learning of life's lessons?

And if people say they don't pity her, why isn't there anything set up in our society to honor and validate such a person? Why are there only traditions that celebrate coupling or having children and none to celebrate all the aspects of being a man or a woman?

Who gives a crap about my opinion? Maybe no one, but letting it out has released some serious pressure build up in me!!! And it has actually made it waaaaaaaaaay easier for me to view others through compassionate eyes. Maybe I'll help someone else do the same. Then, there ya go...there'd be at least two more people bringing a little more peace to the planet, right? That's gotta count for something...that's if you're counting, I guess . But I digress. Back to the show...

Chapter 2
Translating

"So, is there a man in your life?"

Translation = Do you have a life yet? Is your poor pitiful single situation over?

You cannot believe how many times I'm asked that. We're so trained to think of life only on *that* path that most casual conversations start with that very question. Seriously, what does it really mean to the asker? Is this that much of worry for them? If you don't know me enough to already know the answer, then chances are we aren't very close, in which case, why would you care about my marital status? All it really serves to do is make the *askee* feel the need to justify her existence outside of the couple world. Of course, I guess, the conversation could start with "Do you like women?", but either way, it's a conversation I don't care to be in, I'll tell you that. Now if I feel like divulging my relationship status to someone, that's a different story, but even then I'd question my own motivation. Someone could say I'm just being picky, but I'm telling you that when you take all of the things in this book into the context of what one sees and hears over and over again, it's not picky.

I have seen so many wonderful single people, happy about their day, suddenly greeted by someone who stops 'em for a quick chat. First thing…"So are you seeing anyone…yet? We've gotta find you someone." Do you know how deflating that is? I've watched it in action. A person's physical stance totally changes to the negative and the defensive joking and posturing ensues. And this is all accepted as polite small talk. How polite is it to constantly undermine an on-your-own existence? Seriously, the effect is anything but small.

Here's another one I've heard personally and I've heard asked of my friends:

"But you're perfect. What do you mean you're not married?"

Translation = What's *wrong* with you? Why aren't you married? There must be something really *off* with you...or someone else for that matter. Some great deficiency. Like there is nothing slightly off with any married people we know? Some married people reading this will probably be offended by me saying this out loud. Funny how no one thinks it's offensive to say these things to a single person and, more specifically, a single female. After all, the single, older male is a life-long bachelor. What a sexy thing, huh? It's only the woman who becomes the spinster. Seriously, spinster?! The actual sound of that word is as repugnant as its implication.

A few years ago, I had a younger friend who went to inquire about a job in a bridal shop while she was going back to school. She was actually asked by the shop owner "So you just decided not to get married?" She was only 28 at the time!

And here's a goody:

"It must be nice not to have any responsibilities."

Translation = Not responsible. Even though it comes across as footloose and fancy free at first, it always ends up like a backhanded compliment, leaving a mark on your cheek. So, now we venture into the land of Childless Singledom. Watch out. The slope starts to steepen. Not having any responsibilities? Are you kidding me? You mean, if you've consciously chosen to control your sexual life, knowing that a child could always result and making sure that you *and* your partner are ready for that, that's irresponsible?! You mean that someone who can't have children for some physical reason is not responsible for anything? That some might not give anything to have a child...a family...only to be reminded of their lack every single holiday? That adoption is not always an option for someone, especially single who doesn't make $20 million a movie? That these people that often spend time creating a better world for everyone in it by enjoying their life as it presented itself and choosing not to sit home and hide because they do not have children? That they watch out for people everywhere, not just those in their immediate family, because their path took them on a more global route? True, parenting is hard, hard work. It absolutely may be a path that teaches someone about responsibility, but it is by no means the only path.

Did I mention that I don't have kids?   Last year, I bought something at a store owned by an acquaintance of mine.   When I was signing the credit card slip, he joked, "I need you to sign here...sign your life away. I'd asked for your first born, but obviously that's never going to happen." And then he laughed. Totally caught me off guard. There was a teenage boy in the store, too. My immediate response was just a sound, and I was thinking, "You might want to consider never saying that to someone ever again."   But I stopped.   The comment was sooooo insensitive and ignorant that I didn't even want to give it a rating point on the Nielsen scale by responding.

Now I know this guy wasn't saying this out of spite or intended meanness. He's a nice guy with a wife and two kids. Nope...couldn't have been a more perfect example of the complete ignorance (note that "ignore" shares the same root word) of any female situation outside of the Married-with-Children paradigm. I kept thinking that he has no idea why I don't have children of my own. I know some people will think, "Well, he wasn't thinking. Nobody else would say that." And therein lies the reason behind this book—to make people aware that this stuff goes on *all* the time. And it extends way beyond race, religion, and national boundaries.

Now I understand that we all say things out of ignorance at some time in our lives. I've done plenty of it, especially about homosexuality, interestingly enough, when I was young. But once I'm made aware of my limited-exposure thinking, of something I did not even realize before, a perspective I never considered, well, I try adjust my language and thoughts from then on. And again...that's what I'm trying to do here. Point out something that has been overlooked for a very long time and maybe raise the consciousness level of it.

And for any other thoughts that maybe aren't said aloud relating to how we must be doing something wrong:

Who says being in a couple is doing it right? Seriously, think of all of the really dysfunctional relationships out there. Doing it right or wrong has zero to do with whether or not you're part of a couple. The whole idea of right and wrong oozes with judgment anyway. It's a concrete, black-and-white thinking, forcing people into specific categories filled with assumptions that are often far from accurate.

Chapter 3
Holidays & Coupling

Regarding our mainstream celebrations of love and coupling, I'm here to tell you that you cannot compare obtaining a degree with being celebrated as loving or lovable through one of our many *annual* traditions, holidays, and ceremonies. Getting a degree has to do with having the means to do so, i.e. inclination, time, and/or money...period. It does not necessarily have to do with being smarter or more talented than somebody else and certainly has nothing to do with your lovability as a person. Yet, if I bring up the discrepancy of the reward system in our society, I'm often told about a present I received at a graduation party. I'm thought of as bitter or selfish. Jealousy and selfishness have nothing to do with it. Validation has everything to do with it. I believe that we need to evolve from our current reward system.

Being given a present for earning a degree or getting flowers for a theatrical performance, as lovely as that is, is not even in the same ballpark as the rewards received, again I stress, *annually* for coupling or having a child. Engagement parties, wedding showers, weddings, anniversaries, Valentine's Day, Sweetest Day, Mother's Day, Father's Day, couple's discounts, family discounts, Christmas ads for jewelry and cars for a spouse...the list goes on. Seriously, give me one day that has a culturally advertised ceremony for the lovability of a single person without children. Sounds absurd, doesn't it? Why would we do that? After all, what is there to celebrate, right? If they were getting it right, they'd be married...

Maybe a little visual comparison will emphasize my point here.

Example of Love Celebrations: Married Once - 1 Child – 40 Year Span

	1	2	3	4	5	6	7	8	9	10	11	12	13	14	15	16	17	18	19	20	21	22	23	24	25	26	27	28	29	30	31	32	33	34	35	36	37	38	39	40
Valentine's Day	✓	✓	✓	✓	✓	✓	✓	✓	✓	✓	✓	✓	✓	✓	✓	✓	✓	✓	✓	✓	✓	✓	✓	✓	✓	✓	✓	✓	✓	✓	✓	✓	✓	✓	✓	✓	✓	✓	✓	✓
Sweetest Day	✓	✓	✓	✓	✓	✓	✓	✓	✓	✓	✓	✓	✓	✓	✓	✓	✓	✓	✓	✓	✓	✓	✓	✓	✓	✓	✓	✓	✓	✓	✓	✓	✓	✓	✓	✓	✓	✓	✓	✓
Engagement Party	✓																																							
Wedding Shower		✓																																						
Bachelor(ette) Party	✓																																							
Wedding		✓																																						
Anniversary			✓	✓	✓	✓	✓	✓	✓	✓	✓	✓	✓	✓	✓	✓	✓	✓	✓	✓	✓	✓	✓	✓	✓	✓	✓	✓	✓	✓	✓	✓	✓	✓	✓	✓	✓	✓	✓	✓
Baby Shower				✓																																				
Mother's Day				✓	✓	✓	✓	✓	✓	✓	✓	✓	✓	✓	✓	✓	✓	✓	✓	✓	✓	✓	✓	✓	✓	✓	✓	✓	✓	✓	✓	✓	✓	✓	✓	✓	✓	✓	✓	✓
Father's Day				✓	✓	✓	✓	✓	✓	✓	✓	✓	✓	✓	✓	✓	✓	✓	✓	✓	✓	✓	✓	✓	✓	✓	✓	✓	✓	✓	✓	✓	✓	✓	✓	✓	✓	✓	✓	✓
Grandparent's Day																						✓	✓	✓	✓	✓	✓	✓	✓	✓	✓	✓	✓	✓	✓	✓	✓	✓	✓	✓

Example of Love Celebrations: Uncoupled - No Kids - 40 Year Span

1 2 3 4 5 6 7 8 9 10 11 12 13 14 15 16 17 18 19 20 21 22 23 24 25 26 27 28 29 30 31 32 33 34 35 36 37 38 39 40

Valentine's Day
Sweetest Day
Engagement Party
Wedding Shower
Bachelor(ette) Party
Wedding
Anniversary
Baby Shower
Mother's Day
Father's Day
Grandparent's Day

Is it any wonder as the years go by why many singles start to pull back from gatherings? At first you don't notice. Then, the more time passes, the greater the gap for the childless and/or couple-free person. With each year, the invites to others' celebrations keep rolling in. You continue to smile and accept, all the while the recipients of these traditional rewards start getting much younger than you—kids of neighbors, kids of siblings, then kids of those kids, etcetera, etcetera, etcetera.

You find yourself looking for ways to arrive late and leave early 'cuz the events center on things that are just not part of your own life. You can't explain it 'cuz everyone *"wants you there"* to include you, which is nice, but you've started to figure out that an invite does not necessarily mean you're included. It just means you're there.

You're torn. You love them, right? You're supposed to be happy for others, right? But you're beginning to realize that your happiness is important, too, and traditions that continually celebrate *some* while excluding *others* might not actually be as much about happiness and love as we're led to believe.

Mainstream turns a blind eye to the fact that marriage doesn't happen for everyone and that marriages don't always work out so well. I can't quite figure out why we think the only way to love is through marrying someone else. If we would celebrate the soul of the individual person, the total worth of a woman, the total worth of a man, can you imagine the difference that might make on our perception of happiness and peace and how that could elevate *all* of our relationships, knowing that happiness starts as an inside job? You would no longer be honored and valued for only your marital status. Your love and peace would be honored in all of your decisions in both work and play. It would affect everything you do...every relationship, not just the partnered ones, you encounter. The opposite of selfish, celebrating the lovability of your self is the most selfless act you can do.

Many people are single *not* just because they turned someone down. Some have never been asked or have yet to come across a partner situation best for them. Some want to wait until they know themselves better. Some choose to leave really unhealthy relationships where their "partner" wants them to be much less than who they are. There are many reasons, but it seems like it's much easier to lump these folk into the "they are afraid of commitment" or "there is something wrong with them" or "they just chose not to" categories.

Same goes with not having kids. Some people don't have children *not* because they chose not to, but because they can't by nature or injury or even the death of a child.   Some figured they'd wait for a partner that would be a good parent and the situation hasn't presented itself yet. Believe me, I admire and respect good parents, but you are not a lesser adult if kids aren't in your own personal picture.

I think we need to start taking a look at how we honor love in our society. Marriage is rewarded with presents and anniversary celebrations while divorce and even being single can be looked upon as failures. Single people, particularly those of us who have never been married and are over 40, are considered deficient in some way…something must be wrong. The truth is that being single at 40 or getting divorced may be the most right thing you ever do. Longevity of a relationship has nothing to do with the quality of it. It doesn't automatically mean you're any better at relationships than anybody else, just like a degree doesn't mean that you are automatically smarter than anybody else. For some, it can just mean that they put the time in.

Can we not admit that some people stay in a long-term relationship out of fear, not love? Fear of being alone, fear of loss of financial support, fear for physical safety, etc. Yet some of the most loving relationships you'll ever experience last only a few moments. One of my best friends in the world died of AIDS in 1993. I knew him for only two years. I learned so much about love and acceptance from him. Does that count less than someone who has been married for 10 times that long? I always hear people "Aaaaaaw" when they hear that a couple has been married for 70 years. They think it's great. My question is "Is it?" It could be loved filled and that's wonderful. But what if someone has been emotionally or physically abused and is afraid to leave? Or what if there's always been a lack of love but their religion forbids a divorce? Or what if the marriage represented financial security only? Or any other combination of factors that don't necessarily involve love. Some people might get mad at reading this, but I feel someone has to finally say it. After all, people have no problem talking about single people and the reasons for being "all alone."

Alright, how many of you single people have been to a wedding reception where you're finally able to just dance and have fun and not worry about the fact that you're not in a couple and then you hear the DJ announce, "Will all single people leave the floor...married couples only" and proceed to eliminate couples from the floor based on how long they have been married? I know this has the intention of being sweet, but it is far from it in reality. The reality is that there are a myriad of layers of humiliation involved in this exercise, first and foremost for the single people, many of whom might really like to be married and to fit in with the mainstream idea of love, who are "singled" out right away as the poor losers who need to get off of the dance floor even before the interminable couples' love song begins.

It's not about numbers...you can't quantify love...there isn't a ration on love. Don't all of our religions talk about the infinite nature of love? Love is everywhere and in each of us...no one has more than another. It's about whether we allow our love to come to the surface...

Divorce

What is divorce a sign of? Fear of commitment? Getting it wrong? Couldn't it be that some people entered into an *expected* relationship without knowing who they really were, by the dictates of someone else, and are now in a place where they realize that fear was their real bond, not love of the other and certainly not love of self?   In which case, doesn't that represent a pretty big step on the road to maturity? If the divorce allows you to move to a more consciously, loving place, well that could be rewarded instead of chastised, couldn't it? The interesting part of all of this is that it can actually take a short-term marriage to arrive at a more loving place. You can be a totally better person for the marriage, but once you divorce, the entire situation is viewed as a failure and no longer celebrated.

Another intriguing thing about divorce is that no matter how many divorces there are, and some people have more than one, it carries a stigma of failure but…but…BUT is still looked upon as more successful than a person in her 40s who has never been married. *There's obviously something wrong with her or someone else for not snatching her up.* Isn't it possible that, in following your heart to learn about love not in a couple, that the universe could be giving you a special gift…the ability to become whole without having to go through a divorce, for example, which even if good for you, I have been told is always painful? Isn't it possible that each individual someone has ever encountered has helped lead her to this place of the greatest peace and love she's known to date? How can any of those, even the tiniest of relationships, pleasant or unpleasant, *not* be viewed as absolutely vital to who and where she is today? How can you limit one's ability to love and be loved to that of a single long-term partnership, and even then by how many ticks of the calendar we managed to gather together?

If we celebrated the love in each of us regardless of connection to perceived long-term partnerships, don't you think we would all make better, more loving choices in our lives? How could we not?

Look at history…You want to tell me that marriage among the nobles of old was always about love?   I'd say power and political maneuvering more likely. Again, this is not to argue against marriage, but just to say that judging people's ability to be love or be happy based upon their marital status really needs to stop. Don't even get me started on the fantasy of "Happily Ever After" created by the Wedding Business. And believe me, it is a business. The dream wedding that will solve all problems. Very easy to be seduced into a relationship because of this much rewarded ceremony...

Wedding Showers

It seems like wedding showers used to serve in helping young couples start a home together. I can understand how hard it can be to go from your parents' home to your own place when you don't own anything that is needed to function in daily home life. I guess it was presumed that a single person would live at home because it was socially and financially more difficult to live by yourself. Understandable...sort of.

If a single person wants to leave the nest and hasn't *found* someone yet, why do we not think that they could use a frying pan or some dishes, too? It can actually be more difficult to manage a home with one person/one income instead of two, which is more of the way of things nowadays.

Now if you want to give someone a present, more power to you. But to do it solely out of tradition, you gotta admit there's a gap in the logic. Let's face it...wedding showers are no longer limited to practical necessities. I just find it interesting that, even when people have lived on their own for years or are on a second marriage, they'll receive quite a number of shower gifts, including money for trips. But as someone who has lived by herself for years and not married, I'm not sure why someone would think that I don't have a place and I wouldn't enjoy a few new things or money for a trip. Not that I'm asking for a bunch of gifts, but the principle involved here intrigues me when I step back from the automatic tradition and have a look.

I just recently had someone try to explain to me that the wedding and marriage represent a milestone in life...a milestone on the way to adulthood and love that deserves a reward. So...let me get this straight...if I haven't been married, then I'm farther back on the maturity path and therefore don't win the blender? Do you see what I'm getting at here? I have this wonderful friend, divorced many years ago, who told me her theory on wedding gifts in general. She felt that the gifts from showers and weddings were to serve as a consolation prize for when you discover six months later that this married thing was not going to be what the movies promised--a kind of cushion to help the landing after the fall from Cloud Nine. Made me laugh.

People have said that they are just celebrating someone's happiness and that some day it will happen to me. So...you're saying I can't possibly be happy enough yet, but if I'm lucky, someone will swoop in and change all that for me? Or that the only happiness really worth celebrating is that linked to someone else? See what I'm saying here?! It's so slighting. It's not the actual event that's the real issue here. It's the validation of love and life it represents and who it includes and who it does not. And yeah...with this type of messaging all the time, it's not always easy to be happy!

Vacations & Hotels

Don't hold it against single people if they want their own room on group vacations and the like. It's nothing personal. But when you are used to your space, you're used to your space. And we have to pay more to get that space, by the way. Most vacation packages are set up for "double occupancy." Now you could say, that's just business, but that is just one of the millions of tiny messages that link coupling to rewards. I know...I can hear some groaning, but I'm just trying to paint all parts of the picture here. Needing space is not a selfish thing. Everyone needs some breathing room.   Actually, I believe, if everyone had some, the world would be a much more peaceful place.   You'll find that you are more highly attuned to noise and activity and can tell the difference between lively fun and just plain chaos.

Seating in restaurants

Against the back wall around the corner, near the kitchen swinging door...not a window in sight. It's bad enough that everyone stares at you when you're by yourself while dining out, getting the "poor thing" looks, but you get the worst seat in the place where incidentally you have no chance of remedying your eating-out-alone scenario even if you wanted to. At this great little café in Chicago, I once left a $20 tip on a $9 meal 'cuz the waitress sat me in a nice seat in front of a window during dinner time so that I could have a nice view. She refused to take the tip. I explained my immense appreciation for her kindness 'cuz no one had done that for me before. She said she completely understood. Her husband was a chef in a big restaurant downtown, working through all dinners and holidays, so she was usually dining alone. Single people know this feeling well and usually leave really generous tips for their usually very easy meal, non-messy table, and quick turn over, by the way. Can I get an Amen and Hallelujah for the restaurant that gets that?!

You will not believe the number of people who will hover by a single person's table at a busy restaurant 'cuz they have two or more people in their party and feel they therefore deserve the table more. They actually stare at you...or should I say glare at you...until you gulp your food down and leave. I've had couples ask if they can sit at my table. Nothing uncomfortable about that scenario, eh? I've had people come up and ask me to give up my table for them, even in restaurants where you are to wait to be seated. One time I was at coffee shop I frequented, sitting at a small table. I got up to put some cream in my coffee and came back to find that a woman had taken my coat off my chair, shoved my books and food to the side of the table, and claimed my chair and the other one for her and her young son, declaring they shouldn't have to stand. And she really felt justified! Now there were plenty of tables for four occupied by only two people, but she did not bother them. I know people are reading this thinking that was just a one-time-rude-and-crazy-woman experience, but I'm telling you, it's not.

Maybe there should be a coffee shop etiquette manual or something 'cuz I was, again, at a coffee shop at a table for two with a friend. My friend went to the bathroom. Then a little kid came and just picked up the empty chair to take it to another table. "Hey, put that down," I said. "You don't take a chair without asking permission, first of all, and second, it's being used." Next thing you know the mother is consoling him 'cuz he got teary-eared. She loudly said, "It's ok, Sweetie, you didn't know someone was using it." She threw me a couple of eyes full of daggers stares and then wouldn't even look at me the next few times we ran into each other. I realized she was actually mad at me for telling her son he couldn't do something. First of all, I wasn't mean about it, and second...Hello...he didn't ask. Manners?! There were plenty of other tables actually empty to get chairs from, by the way. But that didn't matter. I was now the bitch.

Well, hear ye! Hear ye! You don't ask for, let alone just take, a chair from a table occupied by one person. It's rude and further isolates the person that is already by herself or himself. When someone is at a coffee shop or whatever, she is usually there to be able to see people. If you take the other chair, then no one can sit down with her if the chance occurs. Ask for an empty chair at a table with two people or more, which there always are, no matter how crowded a place may be. They're already with someone—it's no big deal. If no luck, ask the wait staff. Now, if the single person *offers* the chair without any prodding on anyone else's part, that's a different story. But for heaven's sake, let it be from her generosity.

Ultimately, who sits at each table is up to the restaurant owner or manager and how she or he chooses to run the place. If the management permits a party to dine, then it is really nobody else's business as to the size of the party. Just treat each table as its own party regardless of the number of people sitting there. It's the respectful thing to do. Please quit making it even harder for someone to be out alone.

Kids in Restaurants

Thank you, McDonald's, for installing play areas. It established this newly acceptable child-rearing standard that all businesses that serve food also serve as nurseries and playrooms. Seriously, there are places that are meant for adults. There needs to be a perk or two left to becoming an adult. One of them should pertain to a few places that are for adults to eat and have coffee without children running around and screaming, throwing toys everywhere while the parent sits there ignoring them, thinking nobody minds. Let's be frank. Usually kids are only cute if they are well-behaved and, let's face it...your own. Nobody else thinks your kids are adorable while they are running around banging into to everyone else's tables all the time. Yes, kids should be allowed to run and play and be free, but not in every single venue on the planet. Try a park or an athletic field or the moon or better yet, try a McDonald's with a play area...that's what it's for. But please remember that, as a rule, restaurants and family rooms are not synonymous terms.

I love working with kids and run lots of activities to empower them and promote confidence and self-esteem. But Holy Manoli, boundaries are a necessary part of socialization, especially for someone without kids, who *was* able to, as a child, sit in a restaurant or a church without needing to turn it into a Jungle Gym. Now you don't have to agree with me on appropriate child behavior, but at least acknowledge that someone single without kids is going to see the situation differently, and that does not make her a kid-hating, control freak. If anything, she loves them enough to teach them that respect for other people's boundaries gives them permission to respect their own boundaries—something that I see has as an ever-increasing dilemma for our children as our advancing technology continually finds ways to infiltrate their space and bombard them with messages and junk every minute of the day. A little structure and some behavior boundary setting actually do children far more good than harm. It provides them the tools to deal with our chaotic world of superfast information and communication requests. It gives them a real chance to breathe and think.

Dating

Regarding dating and the single woman over 40, we're not scared as we've gotten older, we're just way more true to our authentic selves than we used to be. Don't assume that because a first date doesn't go any further, it's because we're just afraid of being with someone. We're most likely just really attuned to what we like and don't like and don't need to be out with someone 'cuz "it's better than being by myself." We're not all commitment-phobic. Seriously, we know ourselves really well by now. And we're not feeling sorry for ourselves, either. Really. Trust me.

This leads us to getting set up. Qualifications? Anything in common? Physically attractive? Kind? Generous? Oh no...better...they're single! Yay! That's all we need to know! Show of hands from anyone who has ever been set up only to realize within a nanosecond that the great quality the two of you share is that neither of you are married! Just to keep it clear, older and unattached does not equal desperate to surrender all personality likes/dislikes.

I was at a fun little, hoppin' coffee shop, this time in upstate New York, one Saturday night. I was having tea, eating a scone, and reading a really good book. A very nice gentleman from the church choir I sang in approached me to introduce me to his family, which included his very eligible bachelor son whom he had wanted me to meet. It was a very pleasant meeting and then everyone went on their way. Well, eventually the son asked me to dinner. He brought up our first encounter. He thought it was pretty brave and daring of me to be out on *Date Night* by myself in a very public place, contently reading a book.

I remember thinking that it had never occurred to me until that moment that there are people who, although feeling like venturing out of their abode, would choose to stay home alone rather than be seen, and apparently branded, as someone who was not in a couple or could not get a date. Maybe if I was in a "relationship" that everybody knew about or had a ring on my finger, it would not have been a big deal to be seen out alone on this sacred day of the week. Why would did it even stand out? Were single people supposed to give up one of only seven nights of the week just to save face? Was I some bizarre creature that needed to be hidden away to make everyone else feel comfortable? Why should I restrict my movements because I was by myself? Good grief!

Roles in Life

I loved the movie "Dave" where the character played by Kevin Kline talks about the position of President of the United States as a temp job. Cracked me up, but a little light bulb went off at the same time. We all are asked to play many roles in our life. Like in theater, there are no small parts. Every role is important, but the role does not reflect the worth or quality of the actor. If we honored people as people and not just the roles they fell into, wouldn't we get to the heart of *our* matter sooner? And wouldn't there be more love in each of us and therefore more love in our roles that we choose to play at any given time in our lives? Just a thought...

Colleen Clement   ---   Grin & Bare It

Chapter 4
Reporting Live from Outside the Box

I've learned so much about love outside of the box. I've learned so much about compassion for others that are excluded from other boxes, as well. It's funny. At first you don't even know that there is a box. Your life is presented to you as "The Way It Is for Everyone." I planned for the things I was trained to plan for, just like everybody else around me...a boyfriend, a wedding, a family...they were all to provide happiness and they happened to everyone, right?

Well, my childhood took place in a loving home in a relatively safe community, so I had the opportunity to concentrate on school and pursue my talents without worries of physical survival. I loved learning and creating. I loved the exploration involved in studying. My parents encouraged me to do my best and to see the fun in school. I worked hard and did pretty well. I even paid attention in church...really paid attention. That's where I believe I really began to question things and discovered my quest for truth. Questions...quest...questions...quest....hmmmm...explains a lot. Anywhoooo, growing up Catholic, I was exposed to some of the best documented questioners of status quo ever—Jesus, Francis, and Joan, to name a few. I laugh now looking back 'cuz, while I was supposedly following all the rules in my world as I knew them, I was also solidifying my place squarely outside of that damn box.

I loved math and science, had a gift for the arts, played sports, and I tried every day to live by the Golden Rule—Do unto others as you would have them do unto you. Not saying I was mistake-free by any means, but I tried every day to be a better person than I was the day before. Particularly justice-minded, I was not a fan of bullying. I would stand up for kids that were being picked on, as much as I could, even if I was the only one. I developed a pretty strong sense of self and a love for life. Then I hit the teens where social acceptance became most kids' motivator. Well, I wasn't ever asked out on dates, including proms. Since I had that whole academic left brain thing going on pretty good, I had a very follow-the-logic side to me. I just accepted that I must not be looked at in the dating sense…something must be off with me…must not be lovable in that way. How silly…but that's what I did 'cuz everything in my world seemed to equate the matter of lovability with coupling. I was outside of the box but just didn't know it then.

The mainstream societal image of ideal love seems to always be built around a romantic dating experience and a loving marriage with children. It's presented like *this* love has enough room for everyone, but it's interesting to start to see how small *this* love's territory actually is. Take a look at people who fall outside the boundaries of this box of ideal love.

First, let's consider some reasons why someone might not be or not have been married:

- ⇨ Not in love with someone within the acceptable guidelines, i.e. their family's race or religion.
- ⇨ Same gender marriage is "forbidden" in most places.
- ⇨ Waiting for a great partnership, not settling.
- ⇨ Never been asked.
- ⇨ Divorced.
- ⇨ Nuns and priests whose religions require they remain single.
- ⇨ Spouse died.
- ⇨ Died young before having the opportunity to marry.

⇨ Cognitively impaired individuals who rarely do others even worry about as far as dating and marriage is concerned because physical survival is seen as the primary goal.

⇨ People with more extreme physical conditions where, superficially speaking, they fall outside the norms of attractiveness.

Second, let's list some reasons why someone might not have kids:

⇨ Can't physically have children due to genetics, miscarriage, genital mutilation, accident, or injury.

⇨ A child has died.

⇨ Gave a child up for adoption or had child taken away.

⇨ Has not had sex yet.

⇨ Waiting for a partner who would be a good parent/partner.

⇨ Doesn't want children.

⇨ Cannot afford or does not qualify for the adoption process.

It seems that there are quite a few people standing outside of *this* box constructed by the advertised model of love via coupling and childbearing. This leads to a very subtle class system of love.

Greatest Love?

I often hear that the love a mother has for a child the greatest love there is. Greatest love? I would say it can be an example of love, not the *greatest* love. Love is love is love. It's not about greater or lesser. If it were, then it wouldn't really be love, would it? Love is all encompassing. Many would say that I couldn't possibly know this because I've never had a child. But I'm telling you *that's* right smack dab where the fallacy lies! To say that I cannot know the greatest love first suggests that love has a sort of caste system and second suggests that, unless you've had a child, you can only live with a sub-par quality of love in your life. And that's just not true.

Being a parent provides a more advertised path to love, for sure, but it is certainly not the *only* way. Certainly for some, they never realized how guarded their hearts were until they held their little innocent baby in their arms. They feel they would do anything for that child they love so much. Many times it works out great. But we all know of instances where the parent-child relationship resembles *anything* but love. Sometimes that path becomes filled with conditions, strings attached for the "family," instead of unconditional love. Sometimes it's filled with abuse, neglect, or abandonment. As I said, it is a way that has the *potential* to lead to love, but it is not a guarantee and it is not the only path, either. Mother Teresa, Helen Keller, even young Anne Frank...think of people who never had children that obviously held tremendous love for people in their hearts.

As a child, I remember this strange feeling that I was meant to help the children already here. I guess I presumed that meant adoption, but now I can see there are a millions ways to help people that don't involve the direct care of a child under my own roof. A million important ways. I'm in my mid-40s and don't have any children. I feel I've been able to see things differently—the child in all of us—because I wasn't linked to a single family unit. This has enabled me to serve the world from an interesting vantage point.

Did anyone see the movie *"City of Joy"*? I love the character played by Pauline Collins when she talks about her divorce. Originally from England and now operating a small medical clinic in India, she realized that she personally was just plain better at spreading love over a lot of people rather than spending it all in one marriage, one family. Powerful perspective.

Do I feel sad sometimes that I don't have kids as I approach menopause? Well, yes, but it's only because of the constant programming we receive every day in our media where *love* means having your own family or that the greatest love is that of a mother and child. If those messages weren't always around, I wouldn't think about that way. I'd know that I was meant to learn about life and love simply on a different path. But I'm human and I have moments when I let my conscious guard down. I'm getting better at remembering to breathe in the truth and know that there is no one love greater than any other. A rose is a rose. Love is love.

Chapter 6
Practical Wisdom from Singledom

Separate beds, separate wings

If somebody snores...separate wings! Nothing personal, but sleep is important. Separate beds and/or wings could definitely create more peace in the world. Think about it...those epic, romantic moments in cinema where the king returns home from a battle, he runs to his queen, they embrace and make wild, passionate love. Then...then...he's off to his side of the castle and she's off to hers. That's why they never argue...they sleep and rarely see each other.

That's wisdom that a single person can attest to. If you value and enjoy your time by yourself, instead of being caught in the trap of sadness because you're not currently in the mainstream construct of the "happy" couple, you'll realize the infinite well of love and peace that is inside you...in each of us. It's very renewing to spend time by yourself. You don't need to check yourself into a monastery to do that anymore...that's of a time gone by. The walls from the monasteries have come down, the spirituality once only allowed for a few is available for all. It's harder this way probably...it's easier in a way to block out the world by being stowed away on a mountain top faraway. But it's do-able. Create a space that's yours, and, even if you rarely use it, you'll be so much more peaceful knowing it's there. Even if it's only a little cubby hole or a chair that's all your own. And if you have a partner, couldn't that extra peacefulness make your partnership a better one?

Pets

A pet is not the answer for every single person on the planet. Please do not give unasked for kittens and puppies as presents particularly to someone who you feel doesn't "have anyone else in her life." Pets require a rather strong link to a house or apartment. Not everybody wants that. Lots of people like to get out and see people or travel here and there and can't get home to tend the needs of an animal. Plus, there are those of us who don't like leaving an animal cooped up all day by itself, including cats. And think about it, if you really want your friend to not be alone and find a partner, then giving that friend a pet further connecting her to a dwelling which does not have any other humans in it is probably not the best strategy in achieving your goal.

Thinking that a pet will help with the loneliness of the single person further perpetuates the myth that being single is lonely. You should get a pet because you actually *want* the pet and plan to care for it. Loneliness is an inside issue and can't be changed by anything externally. There is a huge difference between being alone and being lonely. Another divorced friend of mine once told me that the loneliest place in the world is lying each night next to a spouse that you don't love 'cuz you thought it was better than being alone.

I'm not saying that single people never want pets or shouldn't have them. Just let us make that decision. I promise you we'll know when and if it's right for us. And it's not that we're too irresponsible to take care of them.   In fact we're very responsible in making sure a situation is not only right for us, but for the animal, too.

Chapter 7
Bathrooms, Politics, & More

Bathroom Etiquette

People really need to rethink the idea of cell phone usage in bathroom stalls. First of all, there's the whole sanitary issue that I feel should be pretty apparent. Second, there's respect and dignity. Lots of pleasant and not so pleasant things occur in bathrooms, wouldn't you agree? While relieving oneself is a natural process, it is not necessarily a public one. The bathroom can provide a necessary respite from the demands of our days, particularly at work. The last thing you need is to have someone carrying on a conference call on speaker phone while you're all menstrual cramped in the adjoining stall! You know of those people that can't relieve themselves if someone is watching, right? Well, the same applies for hearing, especially by unknown male listeners on the other end of a cell phone in a female lavatory! Ugh!!!

Honestly, ladies, we all know how pleasantly the body behaves during "our time of the month." Words like *irritable, painful, explosive,* and *Hell* come to mind. Is it too much to ask to only have to embarrass ourselves in front of the few that happen to physically occupy the restroom with us? Do we have to involve the planet? And, yes, in case you're wondering, that happened to me at work. And, I actually got reprimanded for asking her to take the conference call outside. I mean, seriously, HOLY CRAP! It's hard enough dealing with the patriarchal hierarchy in the workplace, gals. Do we have to bring it into the Ladies

Room? And if the feminine issue doesn't cause you concern, can you say "OSHA"?!

Bathroom Architecture

Full single doors opening in?! What? I concede that you need them to open in just in case someone comes slamming into the stall without knocking and the lock doesn't work…then you can smash the door back for you protection and privacy. Get it…all for it. But the full door swing into the stall which is always too small and opens ¼ inch from the toilet you now need to straddle just to close the door? Who designs these things? And I'm only a size 12. Why not try double swinging doors, which wouldn't have to take up as much of the length of the stall, with a rubber strip to cover the center opening for privacy. Or just make all stalls bigger. Concept!

As for the number, it's actually criminal how few stalls are in the women's bathrooms at stadiums and theaters.   And if this costs more money…who cares?! It's the decent thing to do. I read somewhere once that if men had periods, tampons would be free.   That made me laugh, and then I realized how true it might be. Until you've experienced it, you can't possible realize the lack of respect and dignity present in most ladies' restrooms. If I were President, I'd mandate that all bathrooms had to have at least one designer who is the same gender as the intended user.

Gender Language

Wanna freak people out? Put feminine words in commonly read items that "normally" use the masculine.   People react quite strongly…even violently to the change. They'll invariably point out that the masculine assumes both genders so it doesn't matter. Ok...right here is where you suggest to them to use the feminine if it's no big deal. And whamo! Suddenly, it *does* seem to matter. "It doesn't sound right." Shoot...just try typing "she/he" instead of "he/she" and you'll get people's panties in a twist. For heaven's sake, if EVOO (extra virgin olive oil) can be added to the dictionary, we can certainly come up with a simple pronoun that means both genders and stops the exclusion half of the human race in all of our important documents that affect our history, our present, and our future.

And why do we call people "feminists" if they support women's issues, but we don't call anyone "masculinists" if they support men's issues? Why is it that men and women can share many of the same qualities, but only the females get the separate, negative stigmas (i.e. "bitch," "slut," "spinster," and the newest trendy slam "cougar") while men are thrown into a positive light ("take-charge kind of guy," "playboy," "bachelor," etc.). Interesting...

It's like what my mom was telling me about her mother. No matter what symptoms Grandma had, the doctors would always condescendingly tell her it was nerves. But with Grandpa, they'd always run tests, figuring there must really be something wrong. Nerves?! Well, after a lifetime of being subtly undermined by a system that trains us to basically mock women's issues, teach men to be intimidated by strength in women, expect men to be the ever-all-providers of money and to see themselves as failures if they aren't CEOs by the time they're 30, and hold women responsible for the happiness of every person they've ever met...don't you think we're all probably a little nervous? I mean, Holy Crap, enough already! Give her some medical assistance, not your friggin' condescension!

Ok...so now I must be a man basher, right? Not at all. I'm just a dignity raiser. People have different talents and physical and mental abilities, and where these are concerned, I think we're not created equal and we don't need to be. However, with regard to spirit and dignity, we are all created equal and we all need to be treated as such.

I read somewhere that one way to describe Aquarians (as if there is any doubt at this point as to my sign) is that they love humanity but hate people. Again, laughed out loud. There's definitely an element of truth to that especially during moments when someone calls me a rather nasty name as I suggest that regardless of race, creed, or nationality, most of recorded history includes only half of the human experience—man's half. I never thought about it when I was a kid in school…just accepted what was presented to me. But as I walked farther and farther into female Singledom, the feminine exclusions appeared brighter and brighter until finally I couldn't believe that I had never noticed them.

Isn't that how life works for everything? We're born into a particular scenario with its own set of rules and prejudices that we assume are the same for everyone. We take it as truth, not because we're stupid, but because we haven't experienced anything differently. Our world is just presented so matter-of-factly that we don't question it at first. And sometimes, we're punished if we do.

Then as we grow, we hopefully become exposed to different cultures and different ways of thinking. This exposure can spotlight anything that is not necessarily based in a universal truth. We discover that a lot of the things presented to us might have actually been based in some sort of fear…someone else's perception of reality…not absolute truth. When we realize this, we can choose to keep the same o' same o', or we can choose to think and act differently. But that's a lot easier said than done, as history has shown us many times. The older the thought pattern or tradition and the more wide-spread it is in a culture, the more resistance to change there can be.

It's like when the character played by Allison Janney on *The West Wing*…yes, a TV show…had to spend a day listening to the cartographers' lobby. She freaked out when they showed her what global maps should really look like. The maps she grew up with were drawn to make countries of the northern hemisphere appear bigger than and on top of those in the southern hemisphere. Apparently, it's not true at all. She couldn't even look at the map where South was at the top, even though from space there is no up or down.   It conflicted with everything she thought she knew as true. Did anyone catch that episode? Brilliant.

It's really radical, earth-shaking, if you will, to find out that there might be a completely different way of perceiving something. Look at those people put to death for daring to consider that the world wasn't flat. And that just involved land mass configuration. Once you involve human spirit, dignity, and matters of the heart, whew...that brings up an entirely different set of walls and defenses, which are ironically built to protect us, but like so many things well-intended, become far more confining and imprisoning with their own set of demons and fears. So, what we built to protect ourselves turns into a cage to keep us anything but safe and free.

With that in mind, I'm thinking we need a second volume added to quite a few of the history books out there...you know...for the feminine side of the story. I'm sure that will go over well...

Running for President

Why do candidates always have to have a spouse and kids? People talk about how they need a family so they remember how to vote on issues concerning families, i.e. couples and kids. Do you really think single people can forget about families? We're vividly reminded of them or I should say our lack of them just about everywhere we turn...trust me on this one. And don't the life style demands of the office of the President kind of wreck the life of the kids? Seriously...they'll have Secret Service for the rest of their lives.

Ponder it for a sec...doesn't it make sense to have a single person as President? Imagine how much less money would be spent on Secret

Service altogether. Only have to watch one person. I've heard people say they would be worried about promiscuity if a single person took the oath. Let's just clear this up...being single does not necessarily entail a sexual-free-for-all. It's not like we're just sitting around drooling, chomping at the bit to get some every minute of the day. Trust me, we can and often do go years without it. We are actually able to control ourselves. And, correct me if I'm wrong, but since when has being married deterred anybody in office from having an indiscretion or two? The more I think of it, the more perfect the idea is. Why bring a whole family into it? We single people can do lots of things, even walk and chew gum at the same time. It's not like we're not balanced or stable...

Aaaah, yes. Stability. Now there's a nerve. How many times do you hear comments like, "Oh he's really stable. He's married and owns a home." Really...like no one slightly off their nut ever tied the knot and bought a house. By saying that married people are more stable, we are saying the single people are less stable, which immediately has an emotional overtone to it. What is it that makes one more stable than someone else? Staying a long time in one place, having a balanced work and home life, owning a house, having a pet...? 'Cuz I can think of both married and single people that fit into those parameters. Of course, I can think of both married and single people who don't. It's just a fallacy to say that a married person is more stable. It's a prejudice, actually, and affects the treatment of singletons in many ways...

World Peace

It occurred to me that, despite the fact that we've been talking about world peace for quite a while now, we haven't seemed to even come close to it yet. World peace? World peace? News flash: The World as a planet can handle herself. Nature knows perfectly well how to have balance and peace. We humans are the ones who are having a problem with it. As I see it, it comes down to a matter of word choice.

I believe our use of the term "world" is messing us up 'cuz we don't really know how to define "world." Business World, Theater World, Fashion World, Nonprofit World, Corporate World, Third World, Religious World, Animal World, Wonderful World of Disney. Honestly...do the more than seven billion people on the planet each have the same concept of "world"? My thought would be no. You can be a part of all different kinds of worlds.

Then there's the issue of accountability. "World" sounds so far off in the distance or so huge that it can release someone from any direct, personal responsibility for it. Worlds have rulers, leaders, governments, right? *They* will take care of it. *They* will help us. It's *their* fault. It's far too easy to lose our own sense of individual connection to and our own personal effect upon our world or worlds. Too vague.

Now the term "peace"...we can more easily get a handle on that one, I think. Most would agree it has to do with harmony, balance, absence of conflict, and general love and respect. There are probably some variances on acceptable forms of peace, but most viewpoints, I suspect, would include the idea that ultimate peace on Earth would be where we as people live in harmony with each other and nature and do no harm. Semantics aside, it seems that basic definition of "peace" can be grasped somewhat universally.

So, here's my thought...instead of taking on the whole world, maybe we should just take on our portion of it, humankind, that is: Human Peace, Person Peace, or We-Are-Each-Individually-Responsible-For-The-Peace-In-Our-Lives Peace. Earth will take care of herself with or without us. Her world includes humans, but it is by no means exclusively human. That can make a big difference in our understanding of peace, don't you think? Once we finally admit that, I think we can take this next step. People Peace...now that makes some serious sense to me. Suddenly becomes entirely personal...the *Me* and the *Us*. Can't hide behind *Them* to take care of us anymore.

Aging

One of my favorite moments of the day occurs when I go on to the Internet to have the right-hand side of the screen show me up close and personal some woman's cellulite-filled hip or the apparently ever-horrifying crow's feet magically wiped away to reveal the younger, beautiful, and obviously more desirable woman. It's just a delicious treat to watch this! Try this cream or that procedure to save you from the terrible fate of the female maturation process!!!

I'm so glad these ads can be found on so many websites because I do not know how I would be able to judge someone's looks properly without them. After all, maturing is only the natural, biological design of life, so by all means, please reinforce ideas to make us scrutinize our every cellular flaw and abhor the journey altogether, living only to desire to stay at a certain age which, if we actually did, would mean that we weren't growing, maturing, or living in any way, shape, or form. We would be frozen in time. That's totally attainable and desirable, right? Let us fear with all of our vim and vigor the loss of youth and the advancement of age. Let us not see the beauty of a soul and continue to limit our perception of beauty to that of the superficial and wrinkle-free. Doesn't that just make you feel all warm and fuzzy on the inside?!!! Seriously, HOLY CRAP! What is wrong with us?

Although most of the ads for anti-aging devices prey upon women, I just saw an ad the other day putting its hook into an area of much male insecurity—Hair. There's this nice looking 40-ish guy in a beautiful house. His two cute, loving little girls come into the living room with a box of hair color to cover his grays because they believe Dad deserves to be with someone. He smiles. They hug and giggle. All is well with the world. WHAT?!!!!! First of all, the guy in the ad wasn't even salt 'n peppery yet. Just a couple of grays. The girls were maybe seven and five. Why are they even aware of their dad's grayness as being a factor as to why he is apparently single ('cuz we all know how horrible that would be)? It was sooooooooooooooooooooooooo appalling! I mean, seriously, does anyone else find this even remotely disturbing?

We need to see the beauty of aging. One of its main attributes introduces us to the marvelous concept of *gray*. Gray is really powerful...no more black and white thinking like in our impetuous youth. Gray teaches us that everything is situational and has many different shades and perspectives. When respected and not shunned, gray teaches us tolerance and patience. Something we might do well to remember in our society where we tend to marginalize the elderly from central community activity, put retired individuals out to pasture as if they have nothing more to contribute, and, particularly in the political arena, choose the shiny, youthful exteriors over the wisdom of experience 'cuz it looks better on TV.

Chapter 8
Concluding Thoughts

You might be asking yourself why someone who thinks being single is ok would get upset at some of comments I've referenced in this book. The reason is that we don't live in a society that supports the single person and I think it's time to change that. I've only just recently reached the point where I can recognize why and articulate it. It's all a journey. All of my thoughts and emotions related to my self-worth were tied to a cultural perspective touting coupling, marriage, and children. I am still a little sensitive to it even though I have been working on releasing that tie for quite a while now.

It's a process to let go. It takes years to build these structures we call our lives. It's like a house that you built over the years with a design and materials that you were trained to think of as, and accepted as, the *only* way to build. Then one day it dawns on you that you could rearrange a room, change a color scheme, or perhaps even do a total rehab out of totally different materials. Revelation! But now comes the work to dismantle the old and rebuild. It takes time.

Marriage and coupling can be great ways to learn about love. But that doesn't mean that they are the only ways or they need to be sought every single waking moment of your life. What about the wonderful friendships in your life? Don't they count for anything? Haven't we all known friendships that reach a far greater level of intimacy than some people ever attain with their spouses?

And don't forget that being single doesn't automatically mean rampant sexual activity and scandalous affairs. In fact, doesn't the commonly accepted definition of having an affair include at least one married person? Swinging, swapping, spousal abuse...aren't those terms in reference to *marital* activities? It's just a fantasy to paint marriage as the more moral, stable, or to-be-sought-after way of life. It's just like anything else. If it involves people, there will be those making pleasant decisions and those making unpleasant decisions, as I like to put it.

You know, I've benefited quite a bit from listening to inspirational authors and speakers on my little journey here on Earth. Yet, a few years ago it started to hit me how many of them make references to "your partner" all the time. For as much as these people have helped me, I feel this is now where I can return the favor. I know the intention is good and all, but really, when you're talking about the ways to create more love in someone's life or make a life better and you *only* refer to things that will come up with "your partner," I don't think you realize how immediately excluding that is.

Not all of us have partners all the time or *any* of the time, for that matter. Yet, if we admit that, someone will invariably assume we are not attracting a partner because of something we are projecting blah blah blah, like we're blocked from love. ***Being single doesn't mean we're blocked from anything!*** Actually...being single can be a sign that you are incredibly unblocked to love and indicates that you're not settling for a scenario that involves compromising who you are.

I think we really need to include language in our talks that will help us evolve to a new level in our thinking about love. Why not say things like "And if you happen to have a partner right now, this new process might affect you this way..." or whatever. Do you see the difference? I know it sounds like a picky little detail, but in the grand scheme of things, what seems big usually turns out to be quite small and what seems tiny...humongous.

Finally, I'll drop this lovely little gem I found that changed everything for me. Ready? *There is no finally.* Well, as far as happiness is concerned anyway. Happiness is about now. *Finally* lives in the future...always. *I'll finally be happy when I move here or get this or marry the right guy. She's finally met someone.* If you're always waiting for *finally*, where does that leave you now? It's that happily-ever-after sentimentality that feeds us this illusion through the Finality Diet. You know what I mean?

And since when has reaching a destination ever been the final word in anyone's life anyway...really? Aren't we always finding ourselves on yet another journey? And with that in mind, when has an end to Singledom ever guaranteed anything as far as how life will play out and what you will learn? To judge our lovability, happiness, and worth by whether or not a partner exists for us at any given moment puts limits on our hearts. And it's sooooo not necessary. We all deserve more than that. It's time to take the love we allow now and expand its territory. The universe is a big place. There's more than enough love for everyone if we're open to it.

And as far as this ranting session goes, I'm actually not trying to tell anyone what to do or believe. Just sharing a slightly different take on things...a little insight with some twists and grins along the way. At the very least, this should ignite some rather interesting conversations, don't ya think? Conversations that maybe have been a long time coming. Well, that's all the baring for now. Thanks for listening. I'm Colleen Clement, signing off, from outside of the box.